# HOW DOES IT FEEL?

Published in 2022 by OH!
An Imprint of Welbeck Non-Fiction Limited,
part of Welbeck Publishing Group.
Based in London and Sydney.
www.welbeckpublishing.com

Compilation text © Welbeck Non-Fiction Limited 2022
Design © Welbeck Non-Fiction Limited 2022

ISBN 978-1-80069-172-8

Compiled by: Lisa Dyer
Editorial: Victoria Godden
Project manager: Russell Porter
Design: Tony Seddon
Production: Jess Brisley

A CIP catalogue reference for this book is available from the British Library

Printed in China

10 9 8 7 6 5 4 3 2 1

THE LITTLE GUIDE TO

# BOB DYLAN

HOW DOES IT FEEL?

# CONTENTS

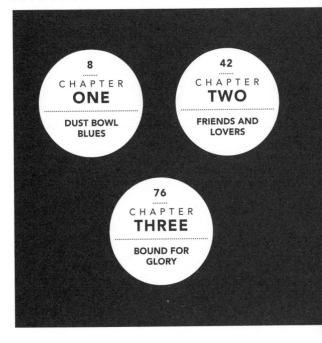

# INTRODUCTION

Having celebrated his 80th birthday in May 2021, with plaudits given around the globe, this influential if enigmatic troubadour-poet has been a'changing with the times since the 1960s when he was the "voice of a generation." Nobel and Pulitzer prize-winner, musician, painter, author, and actor, the living legend's words in lyrics, in print, and in real life have inspired, enthralled, provoked, and puzzled generations of fans, literary buffs, musicians, and songwriters—and have been mulled over by academics and artists alike.

This collection of quotes has been culled from various interviews, features, books, and documentaries over his 60-year career. Humorous, grave, passionate, fearless, surreal, and contradictory, they consist of a rich tapestry of confessions, admonitions, laments, prophecies, and existential meanderings. Interspersed with fascinating facts, *The Little Book of Bob Dylan* can only hope to highlight a few of the deep inner thoughts of the man. The only way to get closer is to listen to the music.

Despite being notoriously secretive and sometimes downright adversarial, Dylan has opened up over the years, revealing his changing influences, beliefs, interests, and music transformations. In "Dust Bowl Blues" you will get a sense of the early hobo-vagabond Dylan, playing on the streets and coffeehouses of New York and the prolific songwriting that spawned hit after hit. His influences, from Little Richard to Guthrie, Baez to the Band, can be seen in "Friends and Lovers", while his uneasy relationship with fame and fate is explored in "Bound for Glory". His ever-evolving career, from folk to electric, country to gospel, is recorded in "A' Changing" and "Music and the Muse" focuses on the art of writing and performing. "Tomorrow Is a Long Time" takes a look at his ideas about life and legacy.

Asked if he felt a sense of pride for influencing music history by Tony Glover in his 1971 unpublished interview, Dylan was his usual impenetrable self: "Yeah, really do, really do feel a sense of pride … on one level. On another level, no, it's nothing at all—of course not."

# CHAPTER
# ONE

# DUST BOWL BLUES

From his Duluth upbringing to the New York City Beat scene, via Woody Guthrie folk ballads and 1960s protest songs, this chapter charts the journey from Robert Zimmerman to Bob Dylan.

I'm a '60s troubadour, a folk-rock relic, a wordsmith from bygone days, a fictitious head of state from a place nobody knows. I'm in the bottomless pit of cultural oblivion.

*Chronicles: Volume One* (2004)

I traveled with the carnival
when I was about 13 years old.
All the way up to when I was 19.
Every year, off and on, I joined
different carnivals.

One of his many invented backstories,
Oscar Brand Radio Show, November 4, 1961

I was born in Duluth—industrial town, shipyards, ore docks, grain elevators, mainline train yards, switching yards. It's on the banks of Lake Superior, built on granite rock. Lot of fog horns, sailors, loggers, storms, blizzards. My mom says there were food shortages, food rationing, hardly any gas, electricity cutting … It was a dark place, even in the light of day.

Bill Flanagan interview, March 22, 2017

You're born, you know, the wrong names, wrong parents. I mean, that happens. You call yourself what you want to call yourself. This is the land of the free.

*60 Minutes*, June 12, 2005

Robert Allen Zimmerman first adopted Dillon as a moniker, legally changing his name to Dylan in August 1962. His Hebrew name is Shabtai Zisel ben Avraham and he's also gone by various sobriquets, including Elston Gunnn, Blind Boy Grunt, Bob Landy, Robert Milkwood Thomas, Tedham Porterhouse, Boo Wilbury, Jack Frost, Sergei Petrov, and even Alias in the film *Pat Garrett and Billy the Kid* (1973).

Some people have many names. I wouldn't pick a name unless I thought I was that person. Sometimes you are held back by your name. Sometimes there are advantages to having a certain name. Names are labels so we can refer to one another. But deep inside us we don't have a name. We have no name. I just chose that name [Dylan] and it stuck.

*Playboy*, January 24, 1978

I'd come from a long ways off and had started from a long ways down. But now destiny was about to manifest itself. I felt like it was looking right at me and nobody else.

*Chronicles: Volume One* (2004)

Destiny is a feeling you have that you know something about yourself nobody else does. The picture you have in your own mind of what you're about will come true. It's a kind of a thing you kind of have to keep to your own self, because it's a fragile feeling, and you put it out there, then someone will kill it. It's best to keep that all inside.

*The Bob Dylan Scrapbook: 1956–1966* (2005)

Shadow Blasters was his first band, formed in high school in Hibbing, Minnesota, in which he emulated a Little Richard style of banging the piano keys.

Next was the Golden Chords, covering Buddy Holly and Eddie Cochran songs for local dances. Rock Boppers followed with an alter ego named Elston Gunnn (with three "n"s), a name under which he secured a gig with Bobby Vee and the Shadows.

The thing about rock'n'roll is that for me anyway it wasn't enough ... the songs weren't serious or didn't reflect life in a realistic way. I knew that when I got into folk music, it was more of a serious type of thing. The songs are filled with more despair, more sadness, more triumph, more faith in the supernatural, much deeper feelings.

Liner notes, *Biograph* (1985)

At the University of Minnesota, Dylan joined the well-known Jewish fraternity Sigma Alpha Mu (Sammy), which included Philip Roth among its brothers (though they were not there at the same time).

He lived at the frat house, performed at a nearby coffeehouse, the Ten O'Clock Scholar, and became involved in the Dinkytown folk scene.

In my 20s and 30s I hadn't been anywhere. Since then I've been all over the world, I've seen oracles and wishing wells. When I was young there were a lot of signs along the way that I couldn't interpret, they were there and I saw them, but they were mystifying. Now when I look back, I can see them for what they were, what they meant.

Bill Flanagan interview, March 22, 2017

I put one on the turntable and when the needle dropped, I was stunned—didn't know if I was stoned or straight … All these songs together, one after another, made my head spin. It made me want to gasp. It was like the land parted.

On listening to Woody Guthrie for the first time, *Chronicles: Volume One* (2004)

To me, Woody Guthrie was the be-all and end-all. Woody's songs were about everything at the same time … He was saying everything in his songs that I felt but didn't know how to. It wasn't only the songs, though. It was his voice—it was like a stiletto—and his diction. I had never heard anybody sing like that.

*Los Angeles Times*, April 4, 2004

I didn't want to see the atomic bathrooms and electronic bedrooms and souped-up can-openers; I wanted to watch and feel the people and the dust and the ditches and the fields and fences.

*Daily Mirror*, September 12, 1963

**66**

I think it's the land. The streams, the forests, the vast emptiness. The land created me. I'm wild and lonesome. Even as I travel the cities, I'm more at home in the vacant lots. But I have a love for humankind, a love of truth, and a love of justice. I think I have a dualistic nature.

**99**

*Sunday Times*, April 25, 2009

Talent-spotter and record producer John Hammond signed Dylan to his first recording contract, with Columbia, after seeing him playing the harmonica while accompanying Carolyn Hester on her third album. The eponymous album was recorded in just two afternoons and initially sold only 5,000 copies.

I just played guitar and harmonica … and sang those songs and that was it. He [Hammond] asked me if I wanted to sing any of them over again but I said no. I can't see myself singing the same song twice in a row. That's terrible.

On recording his first album, Edwin Miller interview, September 1962

I can offer songs that tell something of this America, no foreign songs—the songs of this land that aren't offered over TV and radio and very few records.

Pamphlet advertising Dylan's first New York appearance, Carnegie Chapter Hall, November 4, 1961

The times cry for the truth …
and people want to hear the
truth and that's just what they're
hearing in good folk music
today.

*New York Daily News*, October 20, 1963

Because Dickens and Dostoevsky and Woody Guthrie were telling their stories much better than I ever could, I decided to stick to my own mind.

*New York Mirror*, December 9, 1963

x

Folk music creates its own audience. Because you can take a guitar anywhere, anytime. Most of the places we played in the early days were all parties— house parties, rent parties. Any kind of reason to go play someplace and we'd be there.

*Rolling Stone*, November 5, 1987

Sure, you can make all sorts of protest songs and put them on Folkways record. But who hears them? The people that do hear them are going to be agreeing with you anyway. You aren't going to get somebody to hear it who doesn't dig. If you can find a cat who can actually say, 'Okay! I'm a changed man because I heard this one thing—or I just saw this one thing ...'

*In-Beat* magazine, May 1965

If you like someone's work, the important thing is to be exposed to everything that person has been exposed to. Anyone who wants to be a songwriter should listen to as much folk music as they can, study the form and structure of stuff that has been around for 100 years.

*Los Angeles Times*, April 4, 2004

A folk song has over a thousand faces and you must meet them all if you want to play this stuff. A folk song might vary in meaning and it might not appear the same from one moment to the next. It depends on who's playing and who's listening.

*Chronicles: Volume One* (2004)

I used to think that myself and my songs were the same thing. But I don't believe that anymore. There's myself and there's my song, which I hope is everybody's song.

*Newsweek*, February 26, 1968

This here ain't no protest
song or anything like that,
'cause I don't write protest
songs … I'm just writing it
as something to be said, for
somebody, by somebody.

**"**

Introducing "Blowin' in the Wind," on stage at
Gerdy's Folk City, 1962

"Blowin' in the Wind," written in ten minutes in a café, was based on an old spiritual called "No More Auction Block." According to *Rolling Stone* magazine, it is the 14th greatest rock song ever written. "Like a Rolling Stone" is No.1.

66

Morality has nothing in common with politics.

99

*Chronicles: Volume One* (2004)

There's no black and white, left and right to me anymore; there's only up and down and down is very close to the ground. And I'm trying to go up without thinking about anything trivial such as politics. They have got nothing to do with it. I'm thinking about the general people and when they get hurt.

Tom Paine Award speech, Emergency Civil Liberties Union, December 13, 1963

I don't think when I write, I just react and put it on paper. I'm serious about everything I write … What comes out in my music is a call for action.

*The Guardian*, August 22, 1963

Penning the best-known protest, anti-war, and civil-rights anthems of the 1960s, Dylan also made real-life events his themes: the killings of Emmett Till, Medgar Evers ("Only a Pawn In Their Game"), and Hattie Carroll, and the imprisonment of Rubin "Hurricane" Carter.

CHAPTER
# TWO

# FRIENDS AND LOVERS

While Dylan expertly covers the full scope of love in his songs—from resigned and unrequited to doomed and mythical—he acknowledges his indebtedness to those who loved and influenced him.

You can't be wise and in love at the same time.

"

*No Direction Home* documentary (2005)

Well, you need love. You have to have people who love you, you have to have people you can identify with, who are companions, and there has to be love in your corner. Y'know, if you don't have that, well then nothing you do is gonna be satisfying to you.

Matt Damsker interview, September 15, 1978

I think women rule the world and that no man has ever done anything that a woman either hasn't allowed him to do or encouraged him to do.

*Rolling Stone*, June 21, 1984

She was the most erotic thing I'd ever seen ... The air was suddenly filled with banana leaves. We started talking and my head started to spin."

On girlfriend Suze Rotolo, *Chronicles: Volume One* (2004)

Joan Baez is as tough-minded as they come. A truly independent spirit, nobody can tell her what to do if she doesn't want to do it. I learnt a lot of things from her. For her kind of love and devotion I could never repay that back.

MusiCares Person of the Year speech, February 6, 2015

Joan and me could sing together in our sleep … She was so courageous. Self-disciplined. When I first met her, it seemed as if she'd just come down from a meteorite. And she's never changed.

*Rolling Thunder Revue* documentary (2019)

She had a very unusual way of playing the guitar. I have never heard anyone play it the way Joanie did, I tried to practice it but I never could get that style down … She had that heart-stopping soprano voice and I couldn't get it out of my mind.

*Joan Baez: How Sweet the Sound* documentary (2009)

At every point in my life I've had to make decisions for what I believed in. Sometimes I've ended up hurting people that I've loved. Other times I've ended up loving people that I never thought I would.

*The Dominion*, August 2, 1980

Have you ever lain with somebody when your hearts were beating in the same rhythm? A man and a woman who lie down with their hearts beating together are truly lucky. Then you've truly been in love, m' boy. Yeah, that's true love. You might see that person once a month, once a year, maybe once a lifetime, but you have the guarantee your lives are going to be in rhythm. That's all you need.

*Playboy*, January 1978

Famous for his many mysterious romantic relationships, from muse Suze Rotolo and fellow folkie Joan Baez to wives Sara Lownds and Carolyn Dennis, he has at least six children: Jesse, Anna Lea, Samuel, Jakob (of the Wallflowers), and adopted daughter Maria with Sara; and Desiree Gabrielle Dennis-Dylan.

When I first heard Elvis's voice, I just knew that I wasn't going to work for anybody and nobody was going to be my boss. He is the deity supreme of rock and roll religion as it exists in today's form. Hearing him for the first time was like busting out of jail.

*US* magazine, August 24, 1987

I went over my whole life. I went over my whole childhood. I didn't talk to anyone for a week after Elvis died. If it wasn't for Elvis and Hank Williams, I couldn't be doing what I do today.

*Far Out* magazine, October 12, 2020

But Little Richard I grew up with. And he was there before me. Lit a match under me. Tuned me into things I never would have known on my own.

*New York Times*, June 12, 2020

Buddy Holly, Little Richard,
Chuck Berry, Carl Perkins,
Gene Vincent, Jerry Lee Lewis.
They played this type of music
that was black and white.
Extremely incendiary. Your
clothes could catch fire.

*AARP*, February/March 2015

From the first note, the vibrations from the loudspeaker made my hair stand up. The stabbing sounds from the guitar could almost break a window. When Johnson started singing, he seemed like a guy who could have sprung from the head of Zeus in full armour.

**99**

On Robert Johnson, *Chronicles: Volume 1* (2004)

I read *On the Road* in maybe 1959. It changed my life like it changed everyone else's.

John W. Whitehead's *Grasping for the Wind* (2001)

Although they were friends for over 40 years, Johnny Cash and Dylan would collaborate only once, on Dylan's *Nashville Skyline* album (1969).

Bob appeared on the very first episode of the *Johnny Cash Show* in 1969 where they performed "Girl from the North Country" together.

In plain terms, Johnny was and is the North Star; you could guide your ship by him—the greatest of the greats then and now … Truly he is what the land and country is all about. The heart and soul of it personified and what it means to be here.

*Rolling Stone*, October 16, 2003

His repertoire was beyond category. Songs made my head spin, made me want to gasp, for me it was an epiphany. It was like I had been in the dark and someone had turned on the main switch of a lightning conductor.

On Woody Guthrie, *Interview*, February 1986

These songs are some of the most heartbreaking stuff ever put on record and I wanted to do them justice. Now that I have lived them and lived through them, I understand them better... These songs are cold and clear-sighted, there is a direct realism in them, faith in ordinary life, just like in early rock'n'roll.

On covering American Songbook standards in *Triplicate* (2017), Bill Flanagan interview, March 22, 2017

Prine's stuff is pure Proustian existentialism. Midwestern mind trips to the nth degree. And he writes beautiful songs.

On John Prine, *Huffington Post*, May 16, 2009

America should put up statues to the Beatles. They helped give this country's pride back to it. They used all the music we'd been listening to, everything from Little Richard to the Everly Brothers. A lot of barriers broke down, but we didn't see it at the time because it happened too fast.

*TV Guide*, September 11, 1976

Rimbaud has been a big influence on me. When I'm on the road and want to read something that makes sense to me, I go to a bookstore and read his words. Melville is somebody I can identify with because of how he looked at life. I also like Joseph Conrad a lot, and I've loved what I've read of James Joyce. Allen Ginsberg is always a great inspiration.

*TV Guide*, September 11, 1976

Seeing Ginsberg was like seeing the Oracle of Delphi. He did not care about material wealth or political power. He was his own kind of king.

*Rolling Thunder Revue* documentary (2019)

**"**

My music comes from two places: white hillbilly music—Roscoe Holcomb, stuff like that—and black blues—people like Son House, Charley Patton, Robert Johnson. These are the two elements I've always related to best, even now. Then, all of a sudden in the '60s, I heard Woody Guthrie, which just blew my mind—what he did with a lyric. So, I stopped everything and learned his songs.

**"**

*Los Angeles Times*, May 22, 1978

66

Hey look, I consider Hank Williams, Captain Marvel, Marlon Brando, the Tennessee Stud, Clark Kent, Walter Cronkite, and J. Carrol Naish all influences. Now what is it—please—what is it exactly you people want to know?

99

To the press, *Village Voice*, March 3, 1965

There is no more Frank. There wasn't before him or isn't after. And he never went away. All those other things that we thought were here to stay, they did go away. But he never did.

On Sinatra, *AARP*, February/March 2015

They brought me down to earth and they lifted me up all in the same moment ... And even at the young age, I felt that life itself was a mystery.

On the Staples Sisters, *AARP*, February/March 2015

Joni Mitchell is in her own world all by herself, so she has a right to keep any rhythm she wants. She's allowed to tell you what time it is.

*Rolling Stone*, November 5, 1987

In 1967 during sessions at Dylan's home in Woodstock and the Big Pink house, Bob and the Band recorded what became *The Basement Tapes* (1975), possibly the world's most famous and heavily bootlegged song demos (many appeared on *Great White Wonder*; see page 140).

There's no way to measure his greatness or magnitude as a person or as a player. I don't think any eulogizing will do him justice. He was that great, much more than a superb musician, with an uncanny ear and dexterity. He's the very spirit personified of whatever is Muddy River country at its core and screams up into the spheres.

On Jerry Garcia, press release, October 8, 1995

It pays to know who your friends are but it also pays to know you ain't got any friends.

*Tarantula* (1971)

CHAPTER
**THREE**

# BOUND FOR GLORY

From championing the working man to being hailed the new messiah, Dylan was more comfortable with being everyman or no-man. His attitude toward fame seemed to be to deny it.

I just haven't really struggled for that. It happened, you know? It happened like anything else happens. Just a happening. You don't try to figure out happenings. You dig happenings. So I'm not going to even talk about it.

On being asked why he's so popular, San Francisco press conference, December 6, 1965

> The world don't need me. Christ, I'm only five feet ten. The world could get along fine without me. Don'tcha know, everybody dies. It don't matter how important you think you are. Look at Shakespeare, Napoleon, Edgar Allen Poe, for that matter. They are dead, right?

*Village Voice*, March 1964

66

All I can do is be me, whoever that is … I'm not going to tell them that I'm the Great Cause Fighter or the Great Lover or Great Boy Genius or whatever. Because I'm not, man. Why mislead them? That's all just Madison Avenue, that's just selling.

99

*In-Beat* magazine, May 1965

I'm through listening to other people tell me how to live my life ... I'm just doing now what I feel is right for me, for my own self.

*People*, November 10, 1975

**"**

I had ambitions to set out and find, like an odyssey or going home somewhere ... set out to find ... this home that I'd left a while back and couldn't remember exactly where it was, but I was on my way there. And encountering what I encountered on the way was how I envisioned it all. I didn't really have any ambition at all. I was born very far from where I'm supposed to be, and so, I'm on my way home, you know?

**"**

*No Direction Home* documentary (2005)

It's not to anybody's best interest to think about how they will be perceived tomorrow. It hurts you in the long run.

SongTalk interview with Paul Zollo, May 1991

Having hits buries a singer in the past. A lot of singers hide in the past because it's safer back there. If you've ever heard today's country music you know what I'm talking about.

*The Independent*, February 7, 2015

I always believed that fame is a curse. I never envied one of the famous people I've known.

GQ magazine, October 13, 2016

Shit, man, I'm only me. You know, that's who I am. We are all the same. No one is on any higher level than anybody else. We've all got it within us, for whatever we want to grasp for.

*People*, February 23, 1976

You're asking questions to
a person who's long dead.
You're asking them to a person
that doesn't exist. But people
make that mistake about me
all the time.

*Rolling Stone*, September 27, 2012

I just feel people put me in a position that I didn't really start out to be in. I like to perform, I like to play, but the rest of it kind of confuses me sometimes. I'm kind of camera-shy. Anyway, I never did like to have my picture taken.

Tim Blackmore interview, Capital Radio, June 15, 1981

What good are fans? You can't eat applause for breakfast. You can't sleep with it.

Robert Shelton's *Bob Dylan: No Direction Home* (1986)

You know, sometimes a person's reputation can be far more colossal than the influence of the person. I don't pay any attention to it anymore.

*Morning Edition*, NPR, October 12, 2004

Dylan scored his first No.1 hit on *Billboard* in 2020 with the 17-minute "'Murder Most Foul," topping No.2 hits "Like a Rolling Stone" (1965) and "Rainy Day Women #12 and 35" (1966), proving he's as relevant today as ever. It made him the oldest artist to score No.1 of new original material.

66

I had no answers to any of those questions any more than any other performer did, really ... for some reason the press thought that performers had the answers to all these problems in the society and you know, like what can ... What can you say to something like that? I mean, it's just kind of absurd.

99

*No Direction Home* documentary (2005)

> **"**
> It's bad luck to look for
> life's guidance to popular
> entertainers. It's bad luck to do
> that. No one should do that.
> **"**

SongTalk interview with Paul Zollo, 1991

Well ... you know, you can influence all kinds of people, but sometimes it gets in the way—especially if somebody is accusing you of influencing somebody that you had no interest in influencing in the first place. I've never given it any mind at all, really. I don't really care to influence anybody at this time, and if I have influenced anybody, what can I say?

*Guitar World*, Issue 31, 1999

I didn't consciously pursue the Bob Dylan myth. It was given to me, by God.

*People*, November 10, 1975

Being noticed can be a burden.
Jesus got himself crucified
because he got himself noticed.
So I disappear a lot.

*Melody Maker*, November 1970

Their expectations are so high, nobody can fulfill them. They can't fulfill their own expectations, so they expect other people to do it for them. I don't mind being put down, but intense personal hatred is another thing.

On critics, *SPIN* magazine, December 1985

The first musician to be awarded the Nobel Prize in Literature "for having created new poetic expressions within the great American song tradition," Dylan did not attend the ceremony on December 10, 2016. Patti Smith accepted the prize in his place, performing "A Hard Rain's a-Gonna Fall" to orchestral accompaniment.

If someone had ever told me that I had the slightest chance of winning the Nobel Prize, I would have to think that I'd have about the same odds as standing on the moon.

Nobel Banquet speech (delivered on behalf of Dylan by the U.S. ambassador), December 10, 2016

CHAPTER
**FOUR**

# A'CHANGING

No one knows who exactly Bob Dylan is, perhaps not even himself. Folkie vagabond, country crooner, electric rocker, born-again Christian: he contains multitudes.

When you feel in your gut what you are and then dynamically pursue it—don't back down and don't give up—then you're going to mystify a lot of folks.

*Rolling Stone*, November 16, 1978

Everyone is a puppet-master.
Everyone likes to control
puppets and pull their strings
and I'm nobody's puppet and
nobody pulls my strings.

*Omnibus*, BBC, 1986

People seldom do what they believe in. They do what is convenient, then repent.

Twitter, May 2, 2020

The only person you have to think twice about lying to is either yourself or to God.

*60 Minutes*, December 5, 2004

**"**

# I don't believe you ... You're a liar! Play it fucking loud!

**"**

Retort to someone calling him "Judas" due to his change
from acoustic to electric guitar, Manchester Free Trade
Hall concert, May 17, 1966

Dylan "went electric" at the Newport Folk Festival on July 25, 1965, backed by the Paul Butterfield Blues Band.

Many folk standard-bearers decried his move as an abandonment of the genre but it proved to be an important turning point in folk rock. Dylan continued to evolve musically.

Carelessness. I lost my one true love. I started drinking. The first thing I know, I'm in a card game. Then I'm in a crap game. I wake up in a pool hall …

When asked why he went rock 'n' roll by Nat Hentoff, *Playboy*, March 1966

But rock 'n' roll was high energy, explosive and cut down. It was skeleton music, came out of the darkness and rode in on the atom bomb, and the artists were star-headed like mystical gods. Rock 'n' roll was a dangerous weapon, chrome-plated; it exploded like the speed of light; it reflected the times …

Bill Flanagan interview, March 22, 2017

66

Folk-music circles were very cold, anyway. Everybody was pretty strict and severe in their attitudes; it was kind of a stuffy scene. It didn't bother me that people didn't understand what I was doing, because I had been doing it long before they were around. And I knew, when I was doin' that stuff, that that hadn't been done before, either.

99

*Rolling Stone*, November 5, 1987

There's nothing so stable
as change.

Robert Shelton's *Bob Dylan: No Direction Home* (1986)

When Joan [Baez] and I sing it
["Blowin' in the Wind"], it's like
an old folk song to me. It never
occurs to me that I'm the person
who wrote that.

*TV Guide*, September 11, 1976

I change during the course of a day. I wake and I'm one person, and when I go to sleep I know for certain I'm somebody else.

*Newsweek,* May 10, 1997

66

I define nothing. Not beauty, not patriotism. I take each thing as it is, without prior rules about what it should be.

99

IMBD.com

The Band had their own sound, that's for sure. When they were playin' behind me, they weren't the Band; they were called Levon and the Hawks. What came out on record as the Band—it was like night and day. Robbie [Robertson] started playing that real pinched, squeezed guitar sound. He had never played like that before in his life.

*Rolling Stone*, October 22, 1987

Born into a Jewish family, Dylan converted to Christianity in 1978 after Messianic Jew Al Kasha prayed with him at a Bible study in Beverly Hills. His "born-again Christian phase" was first captured in music by the 1979 LP *Slow Train Coming*.

By 1981, the phase was over but not the god complex; as he told a reporter when he denied his born-again status, "Jesus himself only preached for three years."

"

Years ago they ... said I was a prophet. I used to say, 'No I'm not a prophet.' They say, 'Yes you are, you're a prophet.' I said, 'No it's not me.' They used to say, 'You sure are a prophet.' They used to convince me I was a prophet. Now I come out and say Jesus Christ is the answer. They say, 'Bob Dylan's no prophet.' They just can't handle it.

"

On tour, Omaha, Nebraska, January 25, 1980

I've never said I'm born again.
That's just a media term. I don't
think I've been an agnostic. I've
always thought there's a superior
power, that this is not the real
world and that there's a world
to come.

*Rolling Stone*, June 21, 1984

Here's the thing with me and the religious thing. This is the flat-out truth: I find the religiosity and philosophy in the music. I don't find it anywhere else. Songs like "Let Me Rest on a Peaceful Mountain" or "I Saw the Light"— that's my religion. I don't adhere to rabbis, preachers, evangelists, all of that … The songs are my lexicon. I believe the songs.

*Newsweek*, October 6, 1997

*Slow Train Coming* was Dylan's first album post conversion to Christianity. Despite its evangelical themes, it went platinum, reaching No. 3 in the U.S. charts, outselling *Blood on the Tracks* and *Blonde on Blonde* in its first year. He released two more religious albums before returning to secular themes of life and love in *Infidels* (1983).

**"**

I'm inconsistent, even to myself.

**"**

*New York Times*, September 28, 1997

People can learn everything about me through my songs if they know where to look. They can juxtapose them with certain other songs and draw a clear picture. But why would anyone want to know about me? It's ridiculous.

On tour, Lincoln, Nebraska, to journalist
Edna Gundersen, August 31, 1990

I was just too stubborn to
ever be governed by enforced
insanity.

*The Fiddler Now Upspoke* (1995)

Greed and lust I can understand, but I can't understand the values of definition and confinement. Definition destroys. Besides, there's nothing definite in this world.

*TV Guide*, September 11, 1976

Nobody knows me and I don't know them. They walk up to me and think they know me because I've written some song that bothered them in a certain way and they can't get rid of it in their mind. It got nothing to do with me.

*Omnibus*, BBC, 1986

# CHAPTER
## FIVE

# MUSIC AND THE MUSE

Credited with starting the idea of the singer-songwriter, that introspective, personalized storytelling, he often simply claims to be channelling something unknown, the universal.

> **"**
> Anything I sing, I call a
> song. Anything I can't sing,
> I call a poem.
> **"**

Liner notes, *The Freewheelin' Bob Dylan* (1963)

If the songs are dreamed, it's like my voice is coming out of their dream.

Robert Shelton's *Bob Dylan: No Direction Home* (1986)

We each have our own vision and a voice inside that talks only to us. We have to be able to hear it.

Jim Jerome interview, October 10, 1975

I just try to be poetically and musically straight. I think of myself as more than a musician, more than a poet. The real self is something other than that. Writing and performing is what I do in this life and in this country. But I could be happy being a blacksmith.

*TV Guide*, September 11, 1976

It's not me. It's the songs.
I'm just the postman. I deliver
the songs.

Robert Shelton's *Bob Dylan: No Direction Home* (1986)

66

You have to be let alone to really accomplish anything.

99

*Newsweek*, February 26, 1968

You don't necessarily have to write to be a poet. Some people work in gas stations and they're poets. I don't call myself a poet because I don't like the word. I'm a trapeze artist.

Nora Ephron and Susan Edmiston interview, August 1965

I consider myself a poet first and a musician second. I live like a poet and I'll die like a poet.

*Melody Maker*, July 29, 1978

It's not that I like it or dislike it; it's what I'm destined to do. Muddy Waters is still doing it, and he's 65. In the States there's a lotta old guys that are doing it, and I kinda feel that when I'm that old, as long as I can do it, I guess I will do it, because it's all I did ever do or want to do.

On being on the road, Craig McGregor interview, March 12, 1978

The words are as important as the melody. Unless you believe the song and have lived it, there's little sense in performing it.

*AARP,* February/March 2015

66

I find it easy to write songs …
If you take whatever there is
to the song away—the beat,
the melody—I could still recite
it. I see nothing wrong with
songs you can't do that with
either—songs that, if you took
the beat and the melody away,
they wouldn't stand up because
they're not supposed to do that,
you know. Songs are songs.

99

*L.A. Free Press*, March 1965

For me it's always been more confessional than professional.

SongTalk interview with Paul Zollo, May 1991

Considered rock's first bootleg album, Dylan's 1969 *Great White Wonder* was the first album produced by the Trademark of Quality (TMQ) record label, in July 1969; the LP took its name from its generic white gatefold cover.

The closest I ever got to the sound I hear in my mind was on individual bands in the *Blonde on Blonde* album. It's that thin, that wild mercury sound. It's metallic and bright gold, with whatever that conjures up.

*Playboy*, March 1978

I'm sure of my dream self. I live in my dreams; I don't really live in the actual world.

Jonathan Cott interview, December 1977

Art is the perpetual motion of illusion. The highest purpose of art is to inspire. What else can you do? What else can you do for anyone but inspire them?

*Rolling Stone*, January 26, 1978

The people in my songs are all me.

*Huffington Post*, May 20, 2009

My songs are personal music; they're not communal. I wouldn't want people singing along with me. It would sound funny. I'm not playing campfire meetings.

*Rolling Stone*, September 27, 2012

Sometimes you say things in songs even if there's a small chance of them being true. And sometimes you say things that have nothing to do with the truth of what you want to say and sometimes you say things that everyone knows to be true. Then again, at the same time, you're thinking that the only truth on earth is that there is no truth on it. Whatever you are saying, you're saying in a ricky-tick way. There's never time to reflect. You stitched and pressed and packed and drove, is what you did.

*Chronicles: Volume One* (2004)

The evolution of song is like a snake with its tail in its mouth.

SongTalk interview with Paul Zollo, May 1991

He's sold 125 million records, making him one of the best-selling musicians of all time. In 2020, he sold his entire back catalogue of 600 songs for over $300m (£225m).

The first two lines, which rhymed 'kiddin' you' and 'didn't you,' just about knocked me out, and later on, when I got to the jugglers and the chrome horse and the princess on the steeple, it all just about got to be too much.

Discussing the song "Like a Rolling Stone" in *Rolling Stone*, September 1988

There's just something about my lyrics that just have a gallantry to them. And that might be all they have going for them. However, it's no small thing.

SongTalk Interview with Paul Zollo, May 1991

I find C major to be the key of strength, but also the key of regret. E major is the key of confidence. A-flat major is the key of renunciation.

*Playboy*, March 1978

'I Contain Multitudes' is more like trance writing. Well, it's not more like trance writing, it *is* trance writing. It's the way I actually feel about things. It is my identity and I'm not going to question it, I am in no position to. Every line has a particular purpose.

On "I Contain Multitudes,"
*New York Times*, June 12, 2020

The song is like a painting, you can't see it all at once if you're standing too close. The individual pieces are just part of a whole.

*New York Times*, June 12, 2020

Dylan has produced five major series of paintings since his first exhibition in 2007 and published eight books of drawings. The covers of *Self Portrait* (1970) and *Planet Waves* (1974) featured his work.

66

I'm not the kind of cat that's going to cut off an ear if I can't do something.

99

Robert Shelton interview, March 1966

I've transcended the pain of material things. I'd be doing what I'm doing if I was a millionaire or not, whether I was getting paid for it or not.

*Newsweek, 1974*

Creativity is not like a freight train going down the tracks. It's something that has to be caressed and treated with a great deal of respect. If your mind is intellectually in the way, it will stop you.

"

*USA Today*, May 5–7, 1995

Just because you like my
stuff doesn't mean I owe
you anything.

IMBD.com

I was sick of the way my lyrics had been extrapolated, their meanings subverted into polemics and that I had been anointed as the Big Bubba of Rebellion, High Priest of Protest, the Duke of Disobedience, Leader of the Freeloaders, Kaiser of Apostasy, Archbishop of Anarchy, the Big Cheese. Horrible titles any way you want to look at it. All code words for Outlaw.

*Chronicles: Volume One* (2004)

People listen to my songs and they must think I'm a certain type of way, and maybe I am. But there's more to it than that. I think they can listen to my songs and figure out who they are, too.

*Rolling Stone*, September 27, 2012

Sometimes the 'you' in my songs is me talking to me. Other times I can be talking to somebody else. If I'm talking to me in a song, I'm not going to drop everything and say, alright, now I'm talking to you. It's up to you to figure out who's who.

*SPIN* magazine, December 1985

My favorite poets are Shelley and Keats. Rimbaud is so identifiable. Lord Byron. I don't know.
Lately if I read poems, it's like I can always hear the guitar. Even with Shakespeare's sonnets I can hear a melody because it's all broken up into timed phrases so I hear it. I always keep thinking, 'What kind of song would this be?'

*Time* magazine, November 25, 1985

Our songs are alive in the land of the living. But songs are unlike literature. They're meant to be sung, not read … And I hope some of you get the chance to listen to these lyrics the way they were intended to be heard: in concert or on record or however people are listening to songs these days. I return once again to Homer, who says, 'Sing in me, oh Muse, and through me tell the story.'

Nobel Lecture speech, posted online, June 5, 2017

# CHAPTER
## SIX

# TOMORROW IS A LONG TIME

Nostalgia, longing, death, and the slipperiness of time are key Dylan themes, and as far as the meaning of life goes, the only thing we know for sure is that we know nothing.

There's no proof of reincarnation and there's no proof of karma but there's a feeling of karma. We don't even have any proof that the universe exists. We don't have any proof that we are even sitting here. We can't prove that we're really alive. How can we prove we're alive by other people saying we're alive?

Jonathan Cott interview, December 1977

We die and are reborn in our own lives many times and yet it is always heading out toward the end which is perhaps the beginning. What do we know about life and death? Nothing!

Philip Fleishman interview, February 1978

You hear a lot about God these days: God, the beneficent; God, the all-great; God, the Almighty; God, the most powerful; God, the giver of life; God, the creator of death. I mean, we're hearing about God all the time, so we better learn how to deal with it. But if we know anything about God, God is arbitrary.

*Rolling Stone*, November 22, 2001

I think of a hero as someone
who understands the degree of
responsibility that comes with
his freedom.

Liner notes, *Biograph* (1985)

I hate debts, especially moral debts. They're worse than money debts.

*New Yorker*, October 4, 1964

In June 2014, Dylan's hand-written lyrics of "Like a Rolling Stone," his 1965 hit single, fetched $2 million dollars at auction, a record for a popular music manuscript.

BBC News

**"**

If I wasn't Bob Dylan, I'd probably think that Bob Dylan has a lot of answers myself.

**"**

*Playboy*, January 1978

There's only one day at a time here, then it's tonight and then tomorrow will be today. 🙺

*Chronicles: Volume One* (2004)

**"**

Chaos is a friend of mine.

**"**

*Newsweek*, December 9, 1985

I accept chaos. I am not sure whether it accepts me. I know there are some people terrified of the bomb, but there are others terrified to be seen carrying a *Modern Screen* magazine. Experience teaches that silence terrifies the most.

*Cosmopolitan*, November 1965

If you try to be anyone but yourself, you will fail; if you are not true to your own heart, you will fail. Then again, there's no success like failure.

*Playboy*, March 1978

A man is a success if he gets up in the morning and gets to bed at night, and in between he does what he wants to do.

*New York Daily News, 1967*

Many of Dylan's songs were hits for other artists, including the No.1s "Mr Tambourine Man" for the Byrds, "All Along the Watchtower" (re-rated from the No.20 spot in 2014) for Jimi Hendrix, and "Blowin' in the Wind" for Peter, Paul and Mary.

I don't think the human mind can comprehend the past and the future. They are both just illusions that can manipulate you into thinking there's some kind of change.

*Sun Sentinel*, September 29, 1995

Sometimes it's not enough
to know what things mean;
sometimes you have to know
what things don't mean.

As Jack Fate in *Masked and Anonymous* (2003)

I'd say people will always believe in something if they feel it to be true. Just knowing it's true is not enough. If you feel in your gut that it's true, well, then, you can be pretty much assured that it's true.

*Playboy*, January 1978

I really thought I'd be seeing Elvis soon.

Commenting on his hospitalization for a heart infection in 1997, Howard Sounes' *Down the Highway* (2001)

I think about the death of the human race. The long, strange trip of the naked ape. Not to be light on it, but everybody's life is so transient. Every human being, no matter how strong or mighty, is frail when it comes to death. I think about it in general terms, not in a personal way.

*New York Times*, June 12, 2020

I had been in a motorcycle accident and I'd been hurt, but I recovered. Truth was that I wanted to get out of the rat race.

*Chronicles: Volume One* (2004)

66

There aren't really any mistakes in life. They might seem to knock you out of proportion at the time, but if you have the courage and the ability and the confidence to go on, well, then ... you can't look at it as a failure, you just have to look at it as a blessing in a way.

99

Robert Shelton's *Bob Dylan: No Direction Home* (1986)

Life isn't about finding yourself or finding anything. It's about creating yourself and creating things.

*Rolling Thunder Revue* documentary (2019)

A cultural icon, he has performed in or been the subject of a film many times, from Peckinpah's *Pat Garrett and Billy the Kid* (1973) and his own *Renaldo and Clara* (1978) to Scorsese's *No Direction Home* (2005) and Todd Haynes' tribute *I'm Not There* (2007).

66

A saint is a person who gives of himself totally and freely, without strings. He is neither deaf nor blind. And yet he's both. He's the master of his own reality, the voice of simplicity. The trick is to stay away from mirror images. The only true mirrors are puddles of water.

99

*Playboy*, March 1978

"Having to pay for sins you didn't commit while all the while you were getting away with murder ... so it all evens out in the end.

Liner notes, *Biograph* (1985)

It's true that a man is his own worst enemy, just as he is his own best friend. If you deal with the enemy within, then no enemy without can stand a chance.

99

*Melody Maker*, July 29, 1978

Apocalyptic is just the end of what would come next, a new beginning. So it's not a negative type word.

*20/20*, October 10, 1985

You must be vulnerable to be sensitive to reality. And to be vulnerable is just another way of saying that one has nothing more to lose. I don't have anything but darkness to lose.

*Rolling Stone*, January 26, 1978